KT-211-645

Look After Yourself
Healthy Teeth

Angela Royston

Heinemann
LIBRARY

www.heinemann.co.uk/library
Visit our website to find out more information about **Heinemann Library** books.

To order:
☎ Phone 44 (0) 1865 888066
🖹 Send a fax to 44 (0) 1865 314091
💻 Visit the Heinemann Bookshop at www.heinemann.co.uk/library to browse our catalogue and order online.

First published in Great Britain by Heinemann Library, Halley Court, Jordan Hill, Oxford OX2 8EJ, part of Harcourt Education.
Heinemann is a registered trademark of Harcourt Education Ltd.

© Harcourt Education Ltd 2003
The moral right of the proprietor has been asserted.

All rights reserved. No part of this publication may be reproduced, stored in a retrieval system, or transmitted in any form or by any means, electronic, mechanical, photocopying, recording, or otherwise, without either the prior written permission of the publishers or a licence permitting restricted copying in the United Kingdom issued by the Copyright Licensing Agency Ltd, 90 Tottenham Court Road, London W1T 4LP (www.cla.co.uk).

Editorial: Sarah Eason and Kathy Peltan
Design: Dave Oakley, Arnos Design
Picture Research: Helen Reilly, Arnos Design
Production: Edward Moore

Originated by Dot Gradations Ltd
Printed and bound in Hong Kong and China by South China

ISBN 0 431 18022 9
07 06 05 04 03
10 9 8 7 6 5 4 3 2 1

KNOWSLEY SCHOOL
LIBRARY SERVICE

British Library Cataloguing in Publication Data
Royston, Angela
Healthy teeth. – (Look after yourself)
1.Teeth – Care and hygiene – Juvenile literature
I.Title
612.3'11

A full catalogue record for this book is available from the British Library.

Acknowledgements
The publishers would like to thank the following for permission to reproduce photographs: Gareth Boden p.**4**; Getty Images p.**23** (Martin Barraud); Powerstock pp.**10**, **16/17**, **22**, **26**, **27**; Science Photo Library p. **7** (Pascal Goethghelack), p.**8** (BSIP Laurent), p.**11** (BSIP VEM), p.**24** (Hattie Young); Trevor Clifford pp.**5**, **6**, **12**, **13**, **14**, **15**, **17**, **18**, **19**, **20**, **21**, **25**.

Cover photograph reproduced with permission of Bubbles/Pauline Cutler.

The publishers would like to thank David Wright for his assistance in the preparation of this book.

Every effort has been made to contact copyright holders of any material reproduced in this book. Any omissions will be rectified in subsequent printings if notice is given to the publishers.

Knowsley Schools
Library Service

3 804326777010	
Askews	28-Oct-2004
J612.31	£9.50
1461156	

Contents

Words written in bold, **like this**, are explained in the Glossary.

Your body

You have to eat to stay alive. Food gives you energy and other things you need to be healthy. Your tongue and teeth work together to chew up food.

Your teeth break up food into small pieces that are easy to **swallow**. This book is about teeth and how to keep them healthy.

Different kinds of teeth

Your teeth work together to cut and chew food into small pieces. The front teeth are sharp and flat like knives. They are called **incisors**. You use them to take a bite.

The **canines** are long and sharp. They grip the food. The back teeth, called **molars**, are wider with a bumpy top. They grind up the food.

canine

incisor

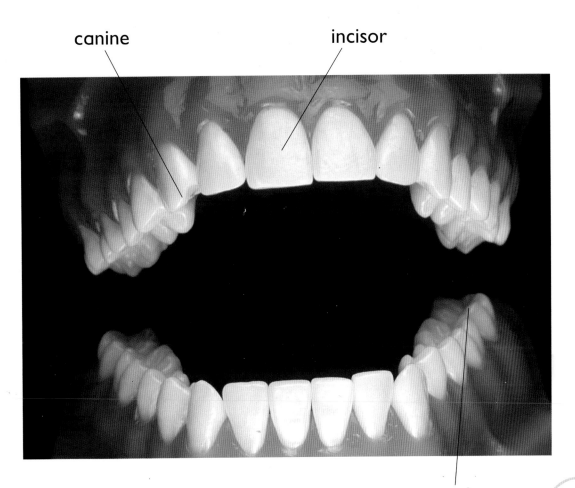

molar

Inside a tooth

Your teeth grow out of your **jaw** bones. The roots are surrounded by your **gums**. You need to look after your gums as well as your teeth.

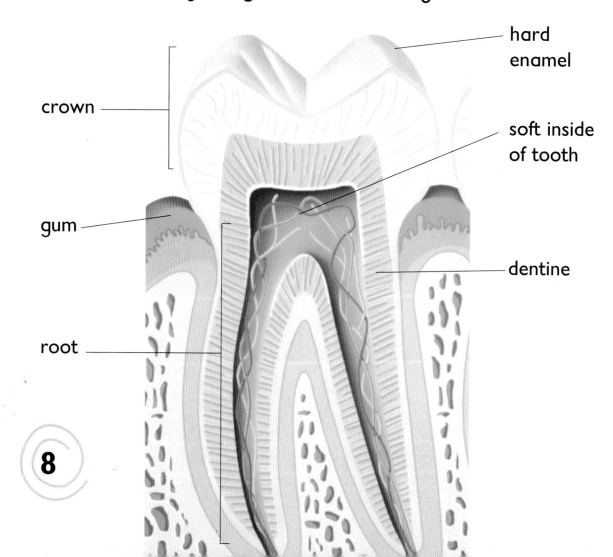

crown

hard enamel

soft inside of tooth

gum

dentine

root

A layer of hard **enamel** covers each tooth. If this enamel wears away, you soon get a hole in your tooth. If the hole is deep your tooth aches a lot.

Sweet and sticky food

Sugar damages your teeth. When you eat something sweet or sticky, some of the sugar sticks to your teeth. **Germs** in your mouth feed on the sugar.

The germs make **acid** that can burn a hole in the **enamel**. When this happens, the hole in the tooth should be filled by a **dentist**.

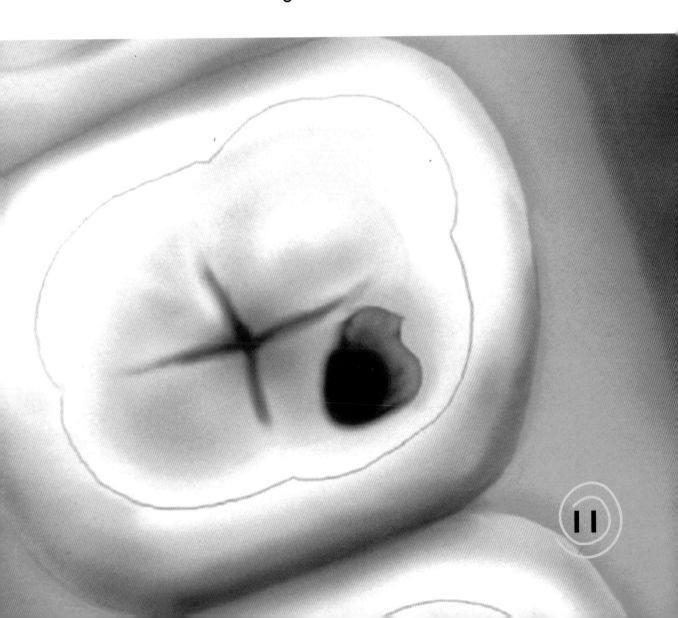

Avoid sweet fizzy drinks

Cola and other fizzy drinks contain a lot of sugar. So does fruit juice. The sugar washes around your mouth and sticks to your teeth.

If you do have a sweet drink, have a glass of water afterwards. The water will wash most of the sugar off your teeth and **gums**.

clean your teeth

You need to clean your teeth at least twice a day. Cleaning your teeth brushes away any bits of food or **germs** that cling to your teeth.

You should clean your teeth before you go to bed and when you have eaten breakfast. Remember not to eat anything after you have cleaned your teeth.

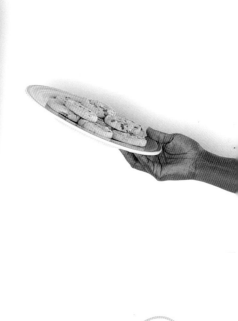

How to brush your teeth

When you clean your teeth, you should brush from the **gum** to the tip of each tooth. Brush the back as well as the front of your teeth.

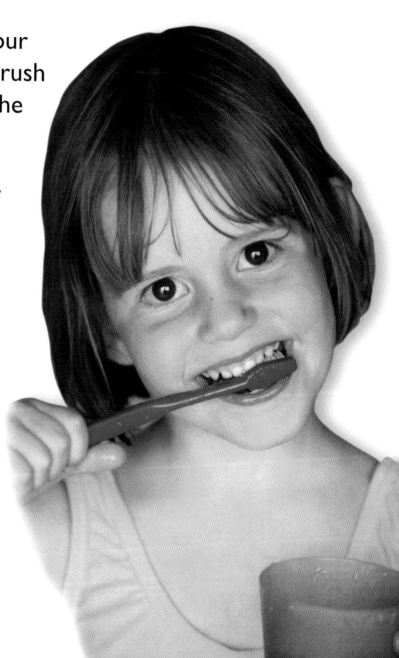

Brushing helps to get rid of food and **germs** between your teeth and under the gums. Finally, brush the tops of the back teeth. Brush your teeth for at least 2 minutes.

17

check your toothbrush!

Your toothbrush will not work properly if the **bristles** are not firm and straight. Check to see if the bristles of your brush are firm, or squashed like these ones.

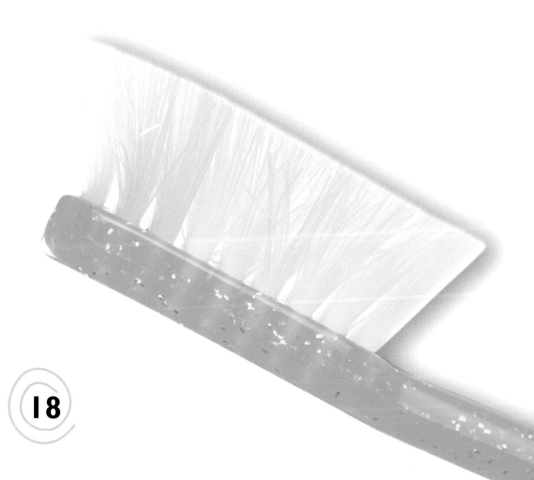

A toothbrush only lasts for a few months.
Then you will need a new one. Make sure that
the brush is the right size for your mouth.

Eat foods that help your teeth

Carrots, apples and other raw fruit and vegetables are good for your teeth. They do not leave lots of sugar in your mouth, as sweets and sugary drinks do.

These foods are also good for your teeth. They contain a **mineral** called **calcium**. Calcium makes your teeth grow strong.

cheese

milk

sardines

Wobble your milk teeth

Your first set of teeth are called milk teeth. When you are aged about five or six years, your milk teeth begin to fall out. They are replaced by bigger teeth.

As your milk teeth become loose, it is a good idea to wobble them. When the milk tooth falls out, it makes more room for the big tooth.

Visit your dentist regularly

You should visit a **dentist** every six months. The dentist will check that your teeth are healthy. If one of your teeth has a hole in it, the dentist will fill the hole.

The dentist will also check that your big teeth are growing well. **Fluoride** makes your teeth stronger. The dentist will check to see if you need extra fluoride.

Look after your big teeth

Big teeth are also called **permanent** teeth. The name shows that these teeth are meant to last. If you lose a big tooth you cannot grow another one.

A big tooth can only be replaced by a false tooth. But if you look after your permanent teeth, they will last for the rest of your life.

Milk teeth and **permanent** teeth begin to form in your **gums** before you are born. Permanent teeth begin to come through as your milk teeth fall out.

It is important to eat foods that contain **calcium**, to make your teeth strong. Foods that contain milk also contain calcium. So do **sardines**, **okra**, **watercress** and white bread.

Your mouth contains millions of **germs**. A substance called **fluoride** makes the **enamel** on your teeth stronger. The enamel becomes so strong that the **acid**, made by germs in your mouth, cannot burn holes in it.

Fluoride makes your teeth particularly strong if you swallow it while your teeth are forming. Some tap water has fluoride added to it. If the water you drink does not contain fluoride you should take fluoride drops once a day.

Most toothpastes contain fluoride. Toothpaste also contains powdered chalk and a kind of soap. The chalk helps to scrub your teeth and the soap makes them clean.

It is important to clean between your teeth. The best way to clean between teeth that are close together is to use **dental floss**. This is a kind of thick thread that you pull backwards and forwards between your teeth. Ask your **dentist** to show you how to use it.

Glossary

acid   chemical that can burn holes in solids such as metals or teeth

bristles   short stiff spikes on a brush

calcium   mineral that makes your teeth and bones strong and hard

canines   four sharp, pointed teeth that you use to bite food

dental floss   stringy tape that is used to clean food out from between the teeth

dentist   person who is trained to take care of teeth and repair damaged teeth

enamel   very hard, glossy substance – each tooth is covered by a layer of enamel

fluoride   mineral that makes your teeth more able to resist decay

germs   tiny living things that attack different parts of the body

gum   flesh that covers your jaw bones and the roots of your teeth

incisors teeth at the front of your mouth that you use to cut food

jaw hinged bone that your teeth grow out of

mineral substance such as calcium present in some foods – your body needs particular minerals to stay healthy

molars wide teeth at the back of your mouth that you use to grind up food

okra vegetable that consists of a sticky green pod

permanent lasting

sardine sea fish, rather like a small herring

swallow push food from your mouth down your throat

watercress plant that can be used in salads and soups

Find out more

Brushing My Teeth by Elizabeth Vogel (PowerKids Press, 2001)

Brushing Well by Helen Frost (Capstone Press, 1999)

Crunch Time Dental Health Programme: All About Us (4Learning, 2000)

Meet Your Teeth by Linda Schwartz (Learning Works, 1996)

Staying Healthy: Dental Care (by Alice B McGinty, Franklin Watts, 1999)

Index

Titles in the *Look After Yourself* series include:

Hardback   0 431 18020 2

Hardback   0 431 18021 0

Hardback   0 431 18026 1

Hardback   0 431 18019 9

Hardback   0 431 18025 3

Hardback   0 431 18024 5

Hardback   0 431 18022 9

Hardback   0 431 18027 X

Find out about the other titles in this series on our website www.heinemann.co.uk/library